T0034627

YUCK, YOU SUCK!

Poems about Animals That SIP, SLURP, SUCK

JANE YOLEN and **HEIDI E. Y. STEMPLE**
Illustrated by **EUGENIA NOBATI**

M Millbrook Press / Minneapolis

This one's for the Dodos (and their littles) —H.E.Y.S.

For Team Stemple, Midwest Division —J.Y.

Dedicated to Checo, the funniest and
most loving dad I could have —E.N.

Poems by Jane and Heidi: pp. 4, 20, 24
Poems by Jane: pp. 6, 7, 16, 17, 18, 26
Poems by Heidi: pp. 8, 10, 12, 13, 14, 19, 22

Text copyright © 2022 by Jane Yolen and Heidi E.Y. Stemple
Illustrations copyright © 2022 by Eugenia Nobati

All rights reserved. International copyright secured. No part of this book may be reproduced,
stored in a retrieval system, or transmitted in any form or by any means—electronic, mechanical,
photocopying, recording, or otherwise—without the prior written permission of Lerner Publishing
Group, Inc., except for the inclusion of brief quotations in an acknowledged review.

Millbrook Press™
An imprint of Lerner Publishing Group, Inc.
241 First Avenue North
Minneapolis, MN 55401 USA

For reading levels and more information, look up this title at www.lernerbooks.com.

Designed by Kimberly Morales.
Main body text set in Hoosker Dont.
Typeface provided by Chank.
The illustrations in this book were created with scanned pencil drawings, textures, and Photoshop
digital painting.

Library of Congress Cataloging-in-Publication Data

Names: Yolen, Jane, author. | Stemple, Heidi E. Y., author. | Nobati, Eugenia, illustrator.
Title: Yuck, you suck! : poems about animals that sip, slurp, suck / Jane Yolen and Heidi E.Y. Stemple ;
   illustrated by Eugenia Nobati.
Description: Minneapolis : Millbrook Press, [2022] | Includes bibliographical references. | Audience:
   Ages 7–11 | Audience: Grades 2–3 | Summary: "This appealingly icky poetry collection presents
   animals that suck—quite literally! From the mosquito to the elephant to the lamprey, discover
   how and why these animals sip, slurp, and suck"— Provided by publisher.
Identifiers: LCCN 2021052059 (print) | LCCN 2021052060 (ebook) | ISBN 9781728415666 (library
   binding) | ISBN 9781728462646 (ebook)
Subjects: LCSH: Animals—Miscellanea—Juvenile literature. | Animals—Food—Juvenile literature.
Classification: LCC QL49 .Y64 2022 (print) | LCC QL49 (ebook) | DDC 590—dc23/eng/20211104

LC record available at https://lccn.loc.gov/2021052059
LC ebook record available at https://lccn.loc.gov/2021052060

Manufactured in the United States of America
2-1010386-49100-11/20/2023

TABLE OF CONTENTS

YUCK, YOU SUCK

Yuck, you suck.
It's not an
insult.
It's a sucker's
intended
result.

You suck up water
to drink, bathe,
swim.
For reasons cute
and reasons
grim.

You sip, you stick,
you eat,
you slurp
without a hiccup, belch, or
burp.

4

Drinking blood, though?
That's just
gross.
But, if you must,
don't over-
dose.

Yuck, you suck.
You really
do.
Yo! Suckers—
we've got
our eyes on
you!

THE GOODS ON THE MOSQUITO

What good is a mosquito,
this bloodsucking "little fly."
I always want to zap her
each time that she zips by.

She's filled up to her eyeballs
With blood from every host.
But I am certain she prefers
MY blood more than most.

I know she's no newcomer.
Her kin were found preserved
in millions-year-old amber.
It's what they all deserved.

DOGGY'S FLEA DILEMMA

Zippety zee,
there's a dog flea on me
and it has bit right through.
It fills itself up
with my blood,
for that's what dog fleas do.
It makes me itch
and scratch a batch.
I wish that it could fly.
For once it left, I'd post a sign:
NO SUCKERS NEED APPLY.
I'm done with being a blood donator.
Flea, I will NOT catch you later.

STINGRAY: THE OCEAN'S VACUUM

He sucks in water,
sand,
and creature.
But
sucking's not
his only
feature.
Once his prey
is caught
inside—
even if it hasn't
yet
died—
like cousin shark,
his deadly teeth
(in his mouth
but underneath)
take over,
chew and chomp and shred,
delicacies—
frog leg,
fish head.

Though you can't see it,
X-rays
have shown,
mollusk, squid—
both shell and bone—
are chewed
and minced,
with stingray zeal,
into a tasty
seafood meal.

BUTTERFLY PUDDLE PARTY
(A CONCRETE POEM)

B
U
T
T
E
R
F
L
Y
.
The
Plant suckers
Need salt.
It's not the fault
Of the plant,
That can't
Provide the butterfly's
needs.

PROBOSCIS.

The
Nectar drinkers
Get salt
Where asphalt
Grooves, dips,
catches, drips.
Supplementing butterfly's
feeds.

REMORAS DON'T (ACTUALLY) SUCK

Remoras don't
suck,
but they're
stuck—
suctioned
tight
with all their
might.
Hangers-on in
ocean
venues,
sampling
from tasty
tasting
menus—
parasites and
skin debris—
eaten
while hitchhiking
through the sea.

JELLYFISH LOCOMOTION

Unlike
any engine
or flipper or fin,
instead of pushing out,
Jelly sucks in.

Professor of movement—
humans take note.
(To avoid getting stung
maybe, stay on your boat.)

The physics is daunting,
this movement of ocean
a vortex created then—
WHOOSH!
Locomotion.

As smart
as anyone on
any terrain—
which is odd,
because Jelly
hasn't a brain.

13

PIGEON'S EVOLUTIONARY BEAK

Flying rat—
I don't think so.
Evolution's made
pigeon a pro.

Compared to others
of his kind,
a better drinker
you won't find.

Most birds scoop,
then tip back drips
in tiny little
birdlike sips.

Pigeon's brilliant
bill is best,
at any avian
drinking test.

His beak works like
a straw in cup.
Just stick it in,
suck water up.

LAMPREYS: BEFORE AND AFTER THE BIG SUCK

FLOWER POWER

It looks like a flower,
with petals of gold.
Keratin fillings.
Oh—beauty—behold!

Get set to go nearer,
through ocean and muck.
Does that flower smell pretty?
'Tis a pity.
Oops.
Suck.

ODE TO A HUNGRY LAMPREY

Blood and fluid.
How do you do it,
you sucker?
It's not pretty,
but it's fast.
Your quick supper
is
their
last.
Say a prayer
for lamprey's prey.
For eons eaten
just this way.

ODE TO THE EREBID MOTH

Oh,
tear drinker,
bird's eye
your
cup.

With your long
proboscis,
you slurp
tears
up!

Nighttime,
near a
Brazilian river.
You alight on
her neck.
Not one
shiver.

Antbird
sleeps
while you
suck
tears.

Her dreams
not filled
with any
fears.

But here's
the fact
that should
arise:
your suck
may damage
that poor
bird's
eyes.

HONEYBEE (A HAIKU)

Nectar all sucked up
Honey sac filled to the brim
Time for hive supper

VAMPIRE BAT'S BAD REPUTATION

Yeah, there's blood,
but I bet a buck
if your money's on bat,
you'll be out of luck.
He licks and laps
but does not suck.

Yeah, there's a victim
and pain endured.
While his bad reputation
remains secured,
there's one thing on which
you can be assured—

he simply does not suck.

ELEPHANT'S TRUNK

An elephant's trunk—
an astounding machine.
It helps every elephant
keep itself clean.

Forty thousand muscles,
all working together.
One giant proboscis
in pachyderm leather.

Sucking up water,
a gallon—or more!
Then, can you guess
what Ms. E has in store?

It's bath time! It's bath time!
Big hip, hip, hooray!
Watch out—
or you just might get
caught in the spray.

BLOODSUCKING LEECH BOTH WAYS

Sometimes we think
leech is a peach.
We use him for purpose
medicinal.

But we're not so delighted
when he sucks, uninvited.
We treat him with hate
unconditional.

YUCK, YOU SUCK REDUX

Hey, suckers,
if you're nice
or
not,
if wings
or stings
are what
you've got,
we're kissing cousins,
you and I.
Whether
slither,
slink,
swim,
or fly.
'Cause mammals, all
are suckers
too.

We start
with milk,
though,
when we're
through,
a simple
straw
will have to do.

ANIMALS SUCK FOR A REASON

(OR, RATHER, MANY REASONS)

Sucking is easy. Even babies do it!

The obvious reason animals suck is for food and water. Human babies, like most mammals, suck milk from their mama or a bottle. Some critters only suck water (pigeons), while others get all their nutrition through sucking (butterflies, stingrays, and lampreys).

But there are other reason animals suck—for protection (remora—more on this later . . .) or for propulsion, which means moving from one place to another (jellyfish). And even to take baths (we see you, elephant).

Some animals (vampire bat) have a sucky reputation even though they don't suck at all. Lots of animals seem to suck, but they actually use different types of behaviors and muscles to move food into their stomachs.

And, though animals with suction cups don't actually suck, they suction (which is different). It seemed fitting to put one suction cup sucker (remora) in this book.

OTHER BOOKS TO SINK YOUR PROBOSCIS INTO

Demas, Corinne, Artemis Roehrig, and Ellen Shi. *Do Jellyfish Like Peanut Butter? Amazing Sea Creature Facts.* Apex, NC: Persnickety, 2020.
Sea creatures do amazing things, but it's not what you may think if you just hear their names. In this question-and-answer book, find out what marine animals really do in the ocean.

Grodzicki, Jenna. *I See Sea Food: Sea Creatures That Look Like Food.* Minneapolis: Millbrook Press, 2019.
Take a look at a variety of ocean animals named for food in this photo book, which features egg yolk jellyfish, chocolate chip sea stars, and many others.

Singer, Marilyn. *Who Are You Calling Weird? A Celebration of Weird and Wonderful Animals.* Lake Forest, CA: Words & Pictures, 2018.
Animals are weird, but they are also cool. Find out about some of the weirdest animals in the ocean, land, and air, and how their oddest qualities help them survive in the wild.

Stewart, Melissa. *Pipsqueaks, Slowpokes, and Stinkers: Celebrating Animal Underdogs.* Atlanta: Peachtree, 2018.
We love to talk about the biggest and strongest animals, but what about the smallest and weakest? Find out how what may seem like problems are really strengths to these animal underdogs.

Writer's Loft Authors & Illustrators. *Friends and Anemones: Ocean Poems for Children.* Sherborn, MA: Writer's Loft, 2020. Discover ocean animals—some that suck and others that do weird things like stick eels up their noses—in this fun book of poetry.

ANATOMICAL TERMS FOR PARTS THAT SUCK

BEAK

Most bird beaks don't work as suckers. Doves (including pigeons) are the only birds that evolved beaks that work this way.

BODY

The jellyfish's body (called a bell) does the sucking to move through the water. As the bell collapses, it forms a sucking vortex of water. This creates an area where water rushes in, moving the jelly forward. Complicated? Yes. And also quite simple.

MOUTH

Either on its own or working with a tongue, many suckers use their mouths to do their sucking. Humans and other mammals suck as babies. Stingrays are mouth suckers too. But they suck up everything in their path before chewing it all to bits.

PROBOSCIS

A long tubular structure that can extend as long or longer than the animal's body. The longest insect proboscis is the Morgan's sphinx moth (*Xanthopan*) that sucks from and pollinates orchids. Its proboscis can reach 1 foot (30 cm) long!

SUCTION CUP

Many animals—frogs, lizards, superheroes—use suction cups to stick to things, but of all the suction cup suckers, the remora is the best. Its suction cup is made up of flexible collagen fibers lined up in a leaflike pattern that adhere to a host's nonsmooth, nonflat surface. And it stays stuck even if the host animal swims fast or jumps out of the water. A true sucking superhero!

TRUNK

An elephant's trunk is actually a proboscis! It's a combination tongue, upper lip, and nose—made up of approximately forty thousand muscles (humans have about six hundred in their entire body). It can lift more than 700 pounds (317 kg) and has one or two fingers at the end (depending on what kind of elephant). It only sucks water up part of the way. Then it spits the water into the elephant's mouth—or into the air!

MORE ABOUT THOSE SUCKERS

MOSQUITO

There are thousands of types of mosquitoes (which means "little fly" in Spanish and Portuguese). These tiny annoyances, from the family Culicidae, grow from egg to larva to pupa. Then the females change into buzzy-winged fliers that use their proboscises to pierce their victims' skin and suck their blood. Even though they only take small amounts, their gross spit causes an itchy bump.

FLEA

Flea is the common name for an insect group that includes twenty-five hundred different species of small flightless bloodsuckers. Fleas don't live very long (at the most about one hundred days), and much less if no blood-filled host—like a dog or human—is around. What makes them go away? They really dislike eucalyptus, lavender, garlic, and citronella—all of which will make a flea flee.

STINGRAY

These odd-looking fish glide through the ocean like graceful underwater birds and then settle on the ocean floor. Don't step on them, though—they don't like it. Also, their tails can be poisonous. Through a small mouth on their belly, they suck in food and shred it into an easily digestible meal with sharklike teeth—which makes sense because they're related to sharks.

BUTTERFLY

The life cycle of these colorful winged insects is made up of egg, caterpillar (larva), chrysalis (pupa), and butterfly. When butterflies are hungry, they uncurl their proboscises to suck from flowers or rotting fruit. When this doesn't give them enough salt or minerals, they do what grown-ups tell you not to—they drink from puddles, which contain the right stuff to complete their diet.

REMORA

These fish are unlikely BFFs with sharks. The ocean predators appreciate the cleanup work their friendly hitchhikers do—eating dead skin and small, pesky, less helpful hangers-on like parasites. The remora isn't stuck by its mouth. Instead, it has a suction cup that evolved from a dorsal fin. This keeps its mouth free to eat those tasty shark leftovers.

JELLYFISH

Jellyfish are not fish. And they don't have brains or bones. Somehow, they are both smart and strong anyway. Many have stinging cells in their tentacles that sting passersby, or worse—kill. But that's mostly for small things they want to eat. Jellyfish don't just float, though. They are master swimmers. Unlike other water creatures, they suck water toward and past them to pull their bodies forward.

PIGEON

These birds have adapted to living in urban (city) environments. While most birds dip their beaks into water, get a drop, and tip their head back to drink, pigeons (and other doves) stick in their strawlike beak and suck. Some people consider pigeons pests, but they are so smart they can recognize themselves in a mirror and understand the alphabet. Still think they are dumb flying rats? Think again!

LAMPREY

These unattractive creatures have survived more than 350 million years without changing much. They are not eels—they are jawless fish with mouths that are always open. Their spiral of teeth and a funnel-like tongue together do the dirty work of sucking and eating pretty much anything in their way. Terrifying? Not always. Some lampreys live their whole lives eating nothing at all. True fact!

MOTH

Like their colorful cousin the butterfly, most moths sip or suck nectar with their big proboscises. However, some moths, such as the erebid moth, feed on tears. If the host (an antbird, for example) isn't producing tears, the moth will scratch its host's eyes until there is a weepy feast. Then the moth sucks up the tears, which is enough to make anyone cry!

HONEYBEE

While male honeybees (drones) hang out, female honeybees use their proboscises to suck nectar from flowers. They store it in their honey sacs (or honey stomachs) before flying back to the hive to feed the other worker bees there. This keeps the hive buzzing. That buzzing, by the way, is not a friendly greeting. It cools the busy hive—and also serves as a warning. Buzz off!

VAMPIRE BAT

Vampire bats have a bad reputation as monstrous bloodsuckers. They are neither. What they are is a subspecies of the leaf-nosed bat—which sounds much cuter. They live mostly in Central and South America. And, like vampires from stories, they do bite with sharp teeth and then lap up (not suck) the blood—mostly from cows, horses, pigs, birds, and the occasional farmer.

ELEPHANT

Elephants (found in Africa and Asia) are the largest living land mammal. They are incredibly smart. Baby elephants are born with short trunks, which they sometimes clumsily trip over. So cute! They learn quickly to use their trunks for sucking up water, making noise, picking up objects (including food), flipping up dust to keep bugs away, and even as snorkels while underwater.

LEECH

These bloodsucking worms have been used by doctors since the Middle Ages (500 to 1500) to try to cure diseases. Gross! While these living, breathing medical devices suck blood out of a patient, they simultaneously release helpful stuff into the patient. Believe it or not, they help prevent things that are actually grosser than leeches—such as blood clots and dead body tissue. How can you tell a leech has sucked your blood? It leaves a small Y-shaped scar. Which probably stands for YUCK, YOU SUCK!

A GLOSSARY OF SCIENCE-Y WORDS THAT DON'T SUCK

AMBER: yellowish tree resin (sticky stuff) that can catch things (like bugs) and preserves them as it hardens, making a fossil. Totally by accident.

AVIAN: like a bird, of a bird, anything, really, having to do with birds

CACHE: a bunch of things you hide away, or the place you hide them

EONS: a really, really, really, really, really long time

EVOLUTION: a super-slow process (think eons) where animals (and humans and birds and bugs and fish) can develop new things (like fins or legs or beaks that sip like a straw) because it's something that makes it easier to live in their habitat

HOST: not the sucker but the suckee—the person or animal that is having blood sucked from them

KERATIN: the stuff that makes hair, nails, horns, feathers, and . . . sometimes scary teeth

LOCOMOTION: moving from here to there

MEDICINAL: used for medicine

MOLLUSK: fancy science word for creatures with soft bodies, no backbone, and usually a shell

NECTAR: sugary plant spit

PACHYDERM: fancy word for elephant

PARASITE: something hanging around (without an invitation) in order to get food

PHYSICS: a subject in school that is about math and science together in a very complicated but very cool way

PRESERVED: to save something, sometimes by accident

PROFESSOR: really smart college teacher

SUPPLEMENTING: adding to what you aren't getting enough of

VORTEX: whirling water or air that pulls things in—stay away!